MY FIRST LITTLE HOUSE BOOKS

MY LITTLE HOUSE SONGBOOK

ADAPTED FROM THE LITTLE HOUSE BOOKS

by Laura Ingalls Wilder

Illustrated by Holly Jones

HARPERCOLLINS*PUBLISHERS*

To my daughter, Gabi

Illustrations for the *My First Little House Books* are inspired by the work of Garth Williams with his permission, which we gratefully acknowledge.

My Little House Songbook was compiled by Erin B. Gathrid.
Jacket illustration by Renée Graef
Music handlettered by Christina Davidson
"Little House"® is a registered trademark of HarperCollins Publishers, Inc.
U.S. Registration No. 1,771, 442.

Some text is adapted from the Little House books by Laura Ingalls Wilder.

My Little House Songbook
Illustrations copyright © 1995 by Holly Jones
Printed in Hong Kong   All rights reserved.

Library of Congress Cataloging-in-Publication Data
    My little house songbook : adapted from the Little house books by Laura Ingalls
Wilder / illustrated by Holly Jones.
        p. of music.   —   (My first little house books)
    Melodies with chord symbols.
    ISBN 0-06-024294-9. — ISBN 0-06-024295-7 (lib. bdg.)
    1. Children's songs.   2. Songs, English.   [1. Songs.]   I. Jones, Holly, ill.
II. Series.
M1997.M9938   1995   94-1999
                                                                           CIP
                                                                          M AC

                    1 2 3 4 5 6 7 8 9 10
                                    ❖
                              First Edition

Once upon a time, a little girl named Laura Ingalls traveled across America in a covered wagon with her Pa, her Ma, her big sister Mary, and her little sisters Carrie and Grace. Laura and her folks lived in many little houses in different parts of the country, and the Ingalls family had lots of wonderful adventures over the years. Some of the happiest times were filled with songs—songs that Pa played on his trusty fiddle, songs that Ma sang to the girls at bedtime, songs that were also games for Laura and her sisters to play with each other, and songs to cheer them up during the hard times, too. Here are some of Laura's favorite songs for you to share with your family in your own little house!

Pop! Goes the Weasel

Traditional

As a special birthday treat for Laura's fifth birthday, Pa played "Pop! Goes the Weasel" for her on his fiddle. He sat with Laura and Mary close against his knees. "Watch," he said, "and maybe you can see the weasel pop out this time."

With pep

A pen-ny for a spool_ of thread, An-oth-er for a nee-dle, That's the way the mon-ey goes, Pop! goes the wea-sel. All a-round the cob-bler's bench, The mon-key chased the wea-sel, The preach-er kissed the cob-bler's wife — Pop! goes the wea-sel!

Yankee Doodle

Traditional

Almanzo and his family had come to town for Independence Day in Father's shining, red-wheeled buggy. In the distance, he heard the band playing. Fifes tooted, flutes shrilled, and the drums came in with a rub-a-dub-dub.

Jaunty

Yan-kee Doo-dle went to town, Rid-ing on a po - ny, He

stuck a feath - er in his hat, And called it mac-a - ro - ni.

Yan-kee Doo-dle keep it up, Yan-kee Doo-dle dan - dy.

Mind the mu-sic and the step and with the girls be han-dy.

America

Samuel Francis Smith and *Henry Carey*

Laura stood next to Carrie and Pa, looking at the American flag. She listened as Pa began to sing and the crowd joined in. How exciting it was to be grown-up enough to come to town on the Fourth of July!

Majestically

My coun-try, 'tis of thee, Sweet land of lib-er-ty, Of thee I sing; Land where my fa-thers died, Land of the pil-grims' pride, From ev-'ry mountain-side Let freedom ring.

Three Blind Mice

Traditional

They kept on singing "Three Blind Mice" until someone laughed and then the song ended ragged and breathless and laughing.

Playfully

Three blind mice, Three blind mice, See how they run! See how they run! They all ran af-ter the farm-er's wife, She cut off their tails with the car-ving knife. Did you ev - er hear such a tale in your life of three blind mice?

Buffalo Gals

Cool White

Grandpa's guests swirled round and round, dancing to Pa's fiddle music. "Grand right and left!" Pa called out. Skirts swished, boots stomped. Laura thought Ma was the loveliest dancer in the world.

BUFFALO GALS

Merrily

As I went lum-b'ring down the street, down the street,

down the street, A love-ly gal I chanced to meet, Oh!

She was fair to view. Buf-fa-lo gals, will you

come out to-night, will you come out to-night, will you come out to-night?

Buf-fa-lo gals, will you come out to-night to dance by the light of the moon?

Oh, Susanna

Stephen Foster

Ma tucked Mary and Laura into bed and laid Baby Carrie beside them. She sat down beside Pa at the fire, and Pa took his fiddle out of its box and began to play, "Oh, Susanna, don't you cry for me."

OH, SUSANNA

Lively

I— went to Cal-i-for-nia with my wash-pan on my
knee; And— ev-ery time I thought of home, I wished it was-n't
me. It— rained all night the day I left, The weath-er it was
dry; The— sun so hot I froze to death, Oh, broth-ers, don't you
cry! Oh, Su-san-na, don't you cry for me! I'm—
going to Cal-i-for-nia with my wash-pan on my knee!

15

Sing a Song of Sixpence

Traditional

Ma opened the oven door, and took out the tin milk pan. It was full of something covered thickly over with delicately browned biscuit crust. She set it before Pa and he looked at it, amazed. "'Sing a song of sixpence—'" said Ma. Laura went on from there, and so did Carrie and Mary and even Grace.

Lyrically

Sing a song of six-pence, a pock-et-ful of rye;
four and twen-ty black-birds baked in a pie!
When the pie was o-pened, the birds be-gan to sing;
was not that a dain-ty dish to set be-fore the king?

Bean Porridge Hot

(From "Pease Porridge Hot")

Traditional

Mary and Laura clapped their hands together and against each other's hands, keeping time while they played Bean Porridge Hot.

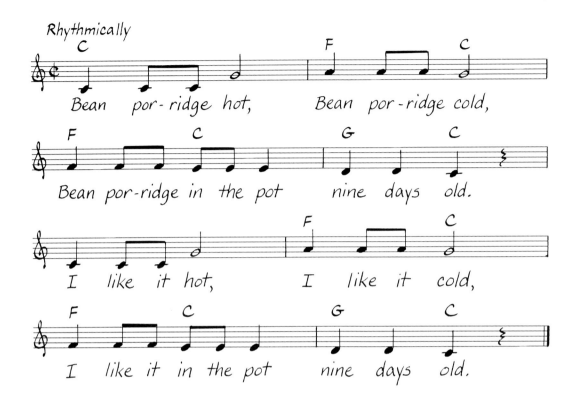

Rhythmically

Bean por-ridge hot, Bean por-ridge cold,

Bean por-ridge in the pot nine days old.

I like it hot, I like it cold,

I like it in the pot nine days old.

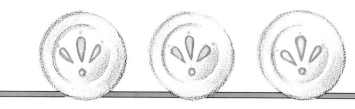

Mary, Put the Dishes On

(From "Polly, Put the Kettle On")

Traditional

Pa glanced at Ma, busy at the stove while Mary and Laura sat listening, and the fiddle slipped into frolicking up and down with his voice. When Laura heard this song, she knew that Mary was to set the table for supper and she was to clear away afterward.

Gaily

Ma-ry, put the dish-es on,   Ma-ry, put the dish-es on,

Ma-ry, put the dish-es on, we'll all take tea.

Lau-ra, take them off a-gain,   Lau-ra, take them off a-gain,

Lau-ra, clear the ta-ble when we've all gone a-way!

Polly-Wolly-Doodle

Traditional

Ma and Pa hoped to buy Mary an organ so that she could keep up with her music. "Bring me my fiddle, Half-Pint," Pa said happily to Laura, "and we'll have a little music without the organ."

POLLY-WOLLY-DOODLE

Heartily

Oh, I went down South for to see my Sal, Sing,
"Pol-ly-wol-ly-doo-dle" all the day! My Sal-ly was a
spunk-y gal, Sing, "Pol-ly-wol-ly-doo-dle" all the day! Fare thee
well, fare-well, fare-well, my fai-ry fay! Oh, I'm
off to Lou'-si-a-na, for to see my Su-sy An-na, sing-ing
"Pol-ly-wol-ly-doo-dle" all the day!

Camptown Races

Stephen Foster

That first winter on Silver Lake, Mr. and Mrs. Boast often came to visit. On those evenings, Pa played the fiddle and everyone sang.

Fast and perky

The Camp-town la-dies sing this song, Doo-dah! doo-dah! The

Camp-town race-track's five miles long, Oh! doo-dah - day! I

come down there with my hat caved in, Doo-dah! doo-dah! I

go back home with a pock-et-ful of tin, Oh! doo-dah - day!

Goin' to run all night! Goin' to run all day! I

bet my mon-ey on the bob-tailed mare And you bet yours on the gray!

Jingle Bells

James S. Pierpont

Christmas Eve had finally arrived! At supper Ma, Pa, and the girls talked about other Christmases they had shared. There had been so many, and here they were again, all together and warm and fed and happy.

Now I Lay Me Down to Sleep

Traditional

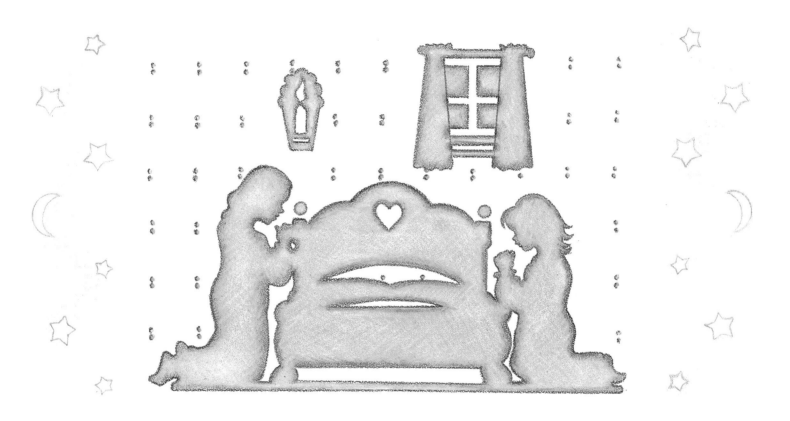

Ma said it was bedtime. She helped Laura and Mary undress and button up their red flannel nightgowns. They knelt down by the trundle bed and said their prayers.

Quietly

Now I lay me down to sleep, I pray the Lord my soul to keep.
If I should die be-fore I wake, I pray the Lord my soul to take.

Home, Sweet Home

John Howard Payne and *Henry Rowley Bishop*

It had been a wonderful day, the most wonderful in Laura's whole life. Today she had gone to town for the first time. Now, as the sun set and the woods darkened, Laura and Mary, Pa and Ma and Baby Carrie were almost home.

Index

of Song Titles and First Lines

A penny for a spool of thread 4

AMERICA (*Little Town on the Prairie*, p. 76) 8

As I went lumb'ring down the street 12

BEAN PORRIDGE HOT (*Little House on the Prairie*, p. 254) 18

Bean porridge hot, Bean porridge cold 18

BUFFALO GALS (*Little House in the Big Woods*, p. 145) 12

CAMPTOWN RACES (*By the Shores of Silver Lake*, p. 212) 24

Dashing through the snow, In a one-hoss open sleigh 26

HOME, SWEET HOME (*Little House in the Big Woods*, p. 176) 30

I came from Salem City with my washpan on my knee 14

JINGLE BELLS (*By the Shores of Silver Lake*, p. 181) 26

MARY, PUT THE DISHES ON (*On the Banks of Plum Creek*, p. 337) 20

Mary, put the dishes on 20

'Mid pleasures and palaces though we may roam 30

My country, 'tis of thee 8

NOW I LAY ME DOWN TO SLEEP (*Little House in the Big Woods*, p.115) 28

Now I lay me down to sleep 28

Oh, I went down South for to see my Sal 22

OH, SUSANNA (*Little House on the Prairie*, p. 332) 14

POLLY-WOLLY-DOODLE (*These Happy Golden Years*, p. 155) 22

POP! GOES THE WEASEL (*Little House in the Big Woods*, p.98) 4

SING A SONG OF SIXPENCE (*Little Town on the Prairie*, p. 104) 16

Sing a song of sixpence 16

The Camptown ladies sing this song 24

THREE BLIND MICE (*By the Shores of Silver Lake*, p. 212) 10

Three blind mice; Three blind mice; 10

YANKEE DOODLE (*Farmer Boy*, p. 175) 6

Yankee Doodle went to town 6